ANIMALS UNDER THREAT

KILLER WHALE

IN DANGER OF EXTINCTION!

Carol Inskipp

Heinemann
LIBRARY

www.heinemann.co.uk/library
Visit our website to find out more information about **Heinemann Library** books.

To order:
☎ Phone 44 (0) 1865 888066
▤ Send a fax to 44 (0) 1865 314091
▯ Visit the Heinemann Bookshop at www.heinemann.co.uk/library to browse our catalogue and order online.

First published in Great Britain by Heinemann Library, Halley Court, Jordan Hill, Oxford OX2 8EJ, part of Harcourt Education. Heinemann is a registered trademark of Harcourt Education Ltd.

Editorial: Sarah Jameson, Nicole Irving and Louise Galpine
Design: Rob Norridge and Jo Malivoire
Picture Research: Laura Durman
Illustration: Stefan Chabluk and Colin Newman
Production: Camilla Smith

Originated by Dot Gradations Ltd
Printed in China by WKT Company Limited

ISBN 0 431 18905 6
09 08 07 06 05
10 9 8 7 6 5 4 3 2 1

British Library Cataloguing in Publication Data
Inskipp, Carol
Killer Whale - (Animals under threat)
599.5'36
A full catalogue record for this book is available from the British Library.

Acknowledgements
The publishers would like to thank the following for permission to reproduce photographs:
ardea.com pp. **32** (F. Gohier), **39** (M. Watson); Bruce Coleman Collection/Pacific Stock pp. **4**, **8**, **17**, **20**; Bruce Coleman Inc. p. **43**; CORBIS pp. **27** (Neil Beer), **38** (Neil Rabinowitz); CORBIS SYGMA p. **31** (Baril Pascal); FLPA pp. **7**, **13** (F. Nicklin/Minden Pictures), **18** (G. Lacz), **23** (A. Visage), **28**, **33** (T. De Roy/Minden Pictures), **36** (M. Newman); Paul Glendell/www.glendell.co.uk p. **35**; Capt. Jim Maya, San Juan Island, WA. p. **37**; NHPA pp. **25** (Stephen Krasemann), **26** (David Currey); OSF/AA pp. **24** (Breck P. Kent), **40** (Richard Kolar); Photodisc: cover header and background image; SeaPics.com pp. **5**, **15** (A. Nachoum), **9**, **19**, **22**, **29**, **41** (I. Visser), **11**, **14** (H. Minakuchi), **16** (R.L. Pitman), **30** (R.W. Baird); Still Pictures pp. **21** (Al Grillo), **34** (Wolfgang Schmidt); WDCS, the Whale and Dolphin Conservation Society p. **42**.

Cover photograph reproduced with permission of FLPA (G. Lacz).

The publishers would like to thank Michael Chinery for his assistance in the preparation of this book.

Contents

Words printed in the text in bold, **like this**, are explained in the Glossary.

The killer whale, or orca

Killer whales, also known as orcas, are sea-living animals with strong, graceful bodies boldly marked in black and white. Although they look like fish, killer whales — along with porpoises, dolphins and other whales — are actually special kinds of **mammals** called **cetaceans** that spend their whole lives in the water.

What are cetaceans?

Like other mammals, such as cows or humans, cetaceans are **endothermic**, or warm-blooded, and feed their young on milk. They also have lungs and need to come to the water's surface to breathe air through one or two nostrils, called blowholes.

Cetaceans are found in all the seas of the world. They have torpedo-shaped bodies and powerful tails that help them swim fast through the water. They can also dive for long periods of time to great depths. Whales are generally the largest in size of the cetaceans and porpoises are the smallest.

There are two kinds of cetaceans: toothed whales and **baleen** whales. Toothed whales use their teeth to catch and hold on to **prey** such as fish, squid and **marine** mammals, before swallowing them whole. They have one blowhole. Killer whales, sperm whales and all dolphins and porpoises are toothed whales.

With their striking black and white markings, orcas are among the easiest cetaceans to recognize.

Baleen whales, on the other hand, have no teeth. They live on very small fish, **plankton** and other tiny living things in the sea. Baleen is a comb-like structure in the whale's mouth that filters food from the water. It is made of keratin, a material like our fingernails. Baleen whales are larger than toothed whales and have two blowholes. Blue and humpback whales are types of baleen whales.

Top predators

Playful and intelligent, killer whales are among the top **predators** in the world's oceans. This means that they hunt and eat other mammals (including whales) as well as fish, and have no natural predators themselves, except humans. Unfortunately, like other cetaceans, killer whales face many threats today and all of these are from humans. Food shortages, **pollution** from chemicals, killing by fishermen and disturbance from boats are some of the problems that are affecting killer whales in the 21st century.

How the orca got its name

Scientists first named the killer whale in 1758. They called it *Delphinus orca* or 'demon dolphin' from the Latin '*delphinus*' meaning 'dolphin' and '*orcus*' meaning 'lower world'. It is not very clear how the killer whale name came about. It may have been because people had seen these whales attacking and killing other whales. Despite their frightening name, killer whales have not been known to attack or kill a human in the wild. The alternative name for killer whale is orca, after its modern scientific name *Orcinus orca*, and this is the name we will use in this book.

Plates of baleen grow from the gums of humpback whales like this one. Water and food enter the mouth and the baleen strains out large numbers of tiny prey at once.

Orca populations

Killer whales, or orcas, live in oceans all over the world. They are some of the most widely distributed **mammals** on earth. They can be found in warm, **tropical** seas as well as cold, **polar** waters, and in coastal bays as well as the open ocean. Sometimes orcas enter river **estuaries**, but they never move far from the sea. Orcas are regular visitors around the coasts of the UK and on rare occasions they visit the warm waters of the Mediterranean. In Australia, orcas live in the waters around Tasmania and they are often seen off the coast of South Australia and Victoria.

Location	Number
Alaska	850
Queen Charlotte Islands	117
Aleutian Islands	
British Columbia	257
Puget Sound	78
Washington State	
California	184
Mexico	65
Greenland	
Norway	3100
Barents Sea	
Iceland	6600
Faroe Islands	
Japan	1900
Papua New Guinea	
North Island, New Zealand	65–167
Argentina	
Crozet Archipelago	43
Australia	
Tasmania	
Antarctica	80,400

NORTH AMERICA · SOUTH AMERICA · ATLANTIC OCEAN · PACIFIC OCEAN · EUROPE · ASIA · AFRICA · INDIAN OCEAN · PACIFIC OCEAN · Mediterranean Sea · Ross Sea

N

- areas of concentrated orca populations
- 65 approximate orca population numbers

Orcas are found throughout the world's oceans, but are concentrated where there are rich sources of food. Unlike some whales, they do not make long journeys.

Because orcas live in all the world's oceans and spend most of their time hidden underwater, it is difficult for scientists to study them easily or guess how large their **populations** actually are. The total world population of orcas is not yet known, but it is possible that there are around 94,000 animals.

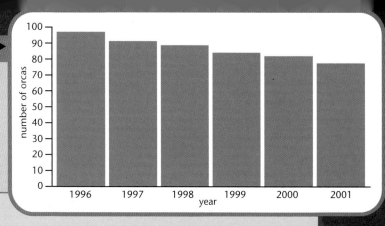

The southern resident population of orcas in Puget Sound, Washington state, USA, declined in number by 20 per cent in the six years up to 2001.

Threatened orcas

Despite the difficulties in studying orcas, two populations of these whales have been closely studied for around 30 years. One population lives off the coast of north-west USA and Canada, and the other lives around the Crozet Archipelago in the southern Indian Ocean. In both populations scientists have found a worrying decline in orca numbers.

In order to study the North American group of orcas more accurately, scientists divide this population into two: whales off the British Columbia coast are known as the 'northern **resident** group'. Those living in Puget Sound, the waters off Washington state and the coast of southern Vancouver are called the 'southern resident group'. A survey of these whales carried out in 2001 showed that the northern resident population had stopped growing after increasing steadily for about twenty years. It was possibly even on the decline. The southern resident population had declined, but no-one knows the reasons why. Along with a fall in the number of the fish that orcas eat, **pollution** and growing disturbance from boats may be the problem here.

The population of orcas around the Crozet Archipelago has also declined dramatically in recent years. Numbers have fallen by more than half in just ten years, from 93 orcas in 1988–89 to only 43 in 1998–2000. Ten years ago orcas in this area lived an average of 60 years, but today they generally live for less than twenty years. In the population that remains there are no young orcas and females of **breeding** age are continually dying. Food shortages and killing by fishermen are possible reasons for this serious decline.

Orcas are most common in the cooler, coastal waters of the Antarctic where the waters are rich in **nutrients** and full of the animals that they like to eat.

The orca body

Orcas have sleek, smooth bodies that glide easily through the water. They are among the fastest **mammals** in the **marine** world and can swim up to 48 kilometres per hour (30 miles per hour). They use this great power of speed to help them catch fast-moving **prey**. The tall **dorsal fin** in the middle of the back keeps the orcas steady in the water and the **pectoral fins** on their sides are used like paddles for steering and stopping.

A breath of air

Whales return to the water's surface regularly to breathe air. Before taking in a fresh breath they blow out a column of moist air, known as a spout or blow, through their blowhole. Like other **cetaceans**, orcas have the amazing ability to control their breathing. Instead of sleeping, they rest by relaxing one half of their brain while guiding their swimming and breathing with the other half. When underwater, special muscles close the blowhole tightly shut to keep water out.

Although orcas can swim fast, they usually move at much slower speeds, about 3–10 kilometres per hour (2–6 miles per hour), about the same walking speed as humans.

A comparison of cetacean sizes.

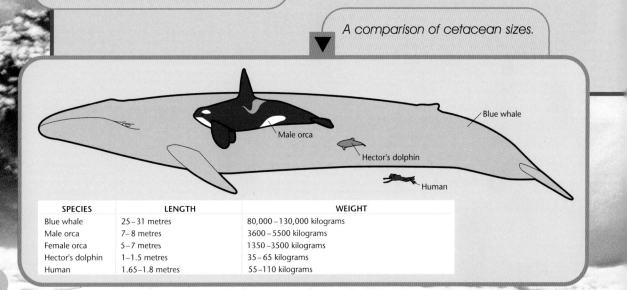

Blue whale

Male orca

Hector's dolphin

Human

SPECIES	LENGTH	WEIGHT
Blue whale	25–31 metres	80,000–130,000 kilograms
Male orca	7–8 metres	3600–5500 kilograms
Female orca	5–7 metres	1350–3500 kilograms
Hector's dolphin	1–1.5 metres	35–65 kilograms
Human	1.65–1.8 metres	55–110 kilograms

Senses

Orcas can hear a huge range of sounds. Although they have ear openings, toothed whales like the orca can receive sounds through the lower jaw. From the jaw, sounds pass to the inner ear, and finally to the brain. Orcas can see fairly well and have skin that is sensitive to touch. Like other whales, orcas have no sense of smell. We do not know whether or not they have a sense of taste.

Hot and cold

Like all **endothermic** animals, orcas need to keep their bodies at a constant temperature. Heat escapes from the body 27 times faster in water than in air. Orcas do not have fur, but like other cetaceans, they have a thick layer of fat under their skin called **blubber**. This acts as an energy store and also helps to keep them warm. Sometimes, when swimming in warmer waters for instance, orcas may become too hot. To cope with this, their large dorsal fin and tail **flukes** contain lots of blood vessels. By pumping hot blood through their fins and flukes, heat can escape more easily from the orca's body, helping it to cool off. Likewise, if an orca feels cold, it pumps as little blood as possible to these areas, and so keeps its body heat in.

Orca tears?

If you look closely at an orca's eye you will see a thick, jelly-like substance oozing out from it. The orca is not crying! This is known as the **mucus** tear and is present in all cetaceans. The mucus, which is slightly oily, helps to protect the orca's eyes and keep them clean.

Communication and orca groups

Orca voices

Orcas make a variety of noises, such as whistles and screams, to communicate with each other. Each orca pod has its own unique range of calls. Some calls are so distinctive that scientists can identify many of them by ear. Orcas can easily recognize their own pod from several kilometres away by the sounds it makes.

Orcas spend much of their time swimming around in dark, murky water, so the use of sound is very important to them for finding their way around, hunting and communicating with each other.

Echolocation

Sound travels through water more than four times faster than through air. When hunting, toothed whales like orcas use sound to tell the position of their **prey**. This is known as **echolocation**. Over recent years, an increase in underwater noise due to human activities, such as shipping and drilling for oil, may be affecting the whales' ability to use echolocation.

Orcas send out high-pitched clicking sounds and listen to differences in the echoes that return. In this way, they can build up a 'sound picture' of their surroundings. Echolocation helps orcas to find their prey.

Sometimes pods join together for a short time to hunt, and up to 250 orcas have been seen swimming together in this way. This pod is swimming in waters off the Canadian coast.

Resident, transient and offshore orcas

Orcas live together in family groups called **pods**. So far, scientists have discovered three distinct types of orca groups, each with different behaviour: they are called the **residents**, the **transients** and the offshores.

Resident orcas stay in one area all the time and form closely-knit family pods numbering five to 25 whales. They usually stay in the pod for life. Residents eat salmon and other fish, which they hunt using echolocation. They call frequently to keep in touch with each other and are known to make twelve different types of sounds. Resident orcas 'talk' to each other more than other orcas and often take part in noisy displays and play.

Transient orcas roam much more widely than residents and are sometimes seen far from the shore. Their pods have less strong family ties and some orcas may leave to join other pods. Transients often form small pods of up to seven whales. They feed on any prey they can find including seals, sea lions, dolphins and other **mammals** as well as sea birds. As their prey generally have good hearing, transients swim quietly and rely on surprise attacks rather than echolocation. For this reason these groups 'talk' to one another less often than resident orcas.

Offshore groups spend most of their time in the open sea, much further away from the shore than other orcas. Very little is known about them. Fish are probably their main **diet**, but they may eat **marine** mammals too. Offshore orcas tend to have many scars on their fins and it is possible that sharks are part of their diet too.

Diet and teeth

Strong swimmers and skilled hunters, orcas play an important role in the **ecosystem** of the sea because they are at the top of the **food chain**. This means that apart from humans, they have no natural **predators**.

The **diet** of orcas is the most varied of all the whales and includes several hundred different animal **species**: squid, fish, sea birds, sea turtles, seals, sea lions, penguins and dolphins. Orcas even hunt and kill other whales. As many as 30 to 40 orcas are known to have made an attack on several hundred narwhals (unusual whales with long tusks). There are records of orcas attacking whales much larger than themselves, such as sperm and humpback whales and even the blue whale. Orcas have also been known to feed on land **mammals**, such as moose, that have been swept out to sea when swimming from one island to another. It is likely that the orca is the only **cetacean** that regularly kills and eats other **endothermic** animals.

Orcas have to eat a large amount of food to help keep them warm. An average-sized orca will eat 250 kilograms of food a day, or 7 per cent of its body weight. Young orcas, called calves, eat around 10 per cent of their body weight each day because they need to grow rapidly.

A hearty meal!

Scientists found the remains of 13 dolphins and 14 seals in the stomach of one killer whale and another held the remains of no less than 32 adult seals!

Killer whale

Seal

Squid

Cod

Plant plankton

This diagram shows how the food chain can work in Europe's North Sea. Both food and energy are transferred up the food chain from plankton at the base to the orca at the top. The arrows indicate that plankton is eaten by cod, cod is eaten by squid and so on up the chain.

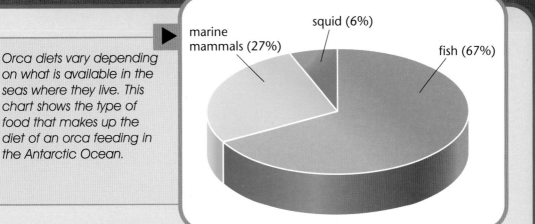

▶

Orca diets vary depending on what is available in the seas where they live. This chart shows the type of food that makes up the diet of an orca feeding in the Antarctic Ocean.

marine mammals (27%)

squid (6%)

fish (67%)

Jaws and teeth

The orca's jaw is wide, with very powerful muscles that help it grasp large, strong **prey** that would otherwise be able to wriggle free and escape. Orca teeth curve inwards and backwards to help catch and grip prey tightly. Orcas use their teeth to bite and tear but they cannot chew. They can swallow penguins and small seals in one go because their throats are so huge!

Orcas have 40 to 52 extremely sharp, cone-shaped teeth that are around 2.5 cm in diameter and nearly 8 cm long.

Tooth tales

On average, orcas in the wild live between 25 and 35 years, although they often reach 50 and some live as long as 80 years! Scientists now use orca teeth to help find out the age of these animals. As an orca gets older it grows more and more layers on the outside of its teeth. If a section of tooth is sliced, the layers can be counted to reveal the orca's age, in the same way that the age of a tree can be found by counting the rings in a cross section of tree trunk.

An efficient hunter

Orcas are highly successful **predators** that usually hunt in groups. By hunting together, orcas are also able to catch animals much bigger than themselves, although they often feed on smaller **prey**. Once a group starts hunting its prey, the animal usually has little chance of escape. As a result the approach of orcas usually panics other **marine** life. Large male orcas often tackle dangerous prey and have even been known to attack great white sharks.

Surprise attack

Orcas use a variety of hunting techniques to catch their prey. In **polar** areas, when an orca finds a seal or bird near the edge of the ice, it sometimes dives deeply and then rushes up to the surface, breaking ice up to a metre thick. The prey slides into the water where the orca catches it.

An orca surges into shallow coastal waters to catch a sea lion in Argentina. Although orcas are often successful in catching prey this way, it can be a dangerous hunting method for them.

On to the beach

In Argentina, orcas have learnt to catch young elephant seals and sea lions on beaches by sliding up into shallow water, catching their prey and then wriggling back into the sea. Orcas also use this dramatic method when hunting young seals around the Crozet Archipelago. Sometimes orcas strand themselves in the shallows and die when hunting like this. When their heavy weight is no longer supported by water, their internal organs start to fail. If stranded out of the water their skin begins to dry out.

Another type of surprise attack is used to catch seals sitting on sheets of floating ice. A group of orcas move forward quickly making a huge wave that splashes over the ice and throws the seal into the water. Sometimes orcas simply use their heads to tip up a floating ice sheet and attack the penguins or seals that fall into the water.

Orcas use other ways of finding food. In the seas around New Zealand orcas search the shallow, coastal waters for large, flat fish called rays that live on the seabed. Around Alaska and in the Indian Ocean, orcas sometimes steal fish that have been trapped on long fishing lines, or longlines, set by fishermen.

Herding fish

Many **cetaceans**, including orcas, catch fish by herding. The orcas swim round and round a shoal, or group, of fish guiding them up to the water's surface. They confuse the fish by flashing the white of their bellies. Once the shoal is tightly grouped, orcas take turns to dash in and seize mouthfuls of fish.

*An orca hunts a shoal of herring in waters off Norway by herding them together. Sometimes orcas slap the fish with their tail **flukes** to stun them.*

In and out of the water

Into the deep

While diving, orcas can save their oxygen and slow down their heartbeat so less blood circulates throughout the body. The blood is then pushed to the brain and lungs where it is most needed. Orcas dive to depths of 30–65 metres in the wild in order to hunt. The deepest recorded orca dive reached 274 metres.

Orcas are among the most exciting **cetaceans** to watch because of their fast, unpredictable movements and inquisitive behaviour. Orcas can be very acrobatic. Some activities seem to have a definite purpose, but scientists do not understand the reasons for all of them. The orcas may sometimes just be having fun!

Orca tricks

Orcas frequently poke their heads vertically out of the water and have a good look around before slipping back silently below the surface. Sometimes a few orcas in a group do this together. This behaviour is known as spyhopping. It is thought that orcas are either locating their **prey** or trying to confuse it.

This orca is spyhopping among the ice in the Ross Sea, Antarctica. Other cetaceans such as pilot whales and grey whales are also known to spyhop.

Orcas often swim upwards at very fast speeds towards the surface so they can jump right out of the water, before landing again with a huge splash. This is called breaching and may be a way of communicating with each other. It may help loosen skin **parasites** or just be another way of playing.

Tail slapping or lob tailing is another favourite orca activity. Orcas do this by sticking their tail **flukes** out of the water and slapping them down hard on the water's surface. It may be used as a warning sign to the rest of the group. The **pectoral fins** can also be raised out of the water and slapped noisily against the surface. When there are many whale-watching boats present in Puget Sound, USA, people have seen mother orcas with young slapping the water repeatedly.

Orcas are famous for their spectacular displays out of the water, especially breaching, where they leap clear of the surface and land on their back or side.

In black and white

The striking black and white patterns on the skin of orcas play an important role, particularly when hunting. Firstly, the bold colouring makes it hard for prey to recognize the complete shape of orcas in the water — a feature that scientists call disruptive colouration because it disrupts, or confuses, the whale's shape.

Secondly orcas are what is called counter shaded. This means that they are mainly dark in colour on top and light below. Any prey swimming above an orca may not be able to tell it apart from the blackness of the water below. Likewise an animal swimming below an orca may look up to see the white orca belly against the light of the sky. Either way, the killer whale's skin patterns help it to 'hide' in the water when hunting.

Breeding

Orcas can **breed** at any time of the year although in northern waters mating is most frequent from May to July. Scientists think that male orcas leave their family groups, or **pods**, for a time to seek out females from other pods in order to mate. Young orcas are called calves.

By swimming close to its mother and often in her wake – the disturbed strip of water behind her – an orca calf can keep up with the pod using the minimum amount of energy.

Orca calves

The calf takes around seventeen months to develop inside its mother and births usually take place in autumn. Male orcas probably never meet their offspring and do not seem to have any part in helping to bring them up.

Growing up

Although male and female calves grow at a similar rate until they are around ten years old, the male eventually grows larger than the female orca.

Like all young **cetaceans**, the orca calf is born underwater. Within seconds of its birth the newborn animal swims to the surface for its first breath of air, helped by its mother's flippers. Within half an hour the calf can swim confidently. A newborn orca calf is around 2 metres long (larger than an adult human) and weighs about 150 kilograms.

Like other **mammals** the calf feeds on its mother's milk, suckling at one of her two teats. The cream-like milk is very rich and contains up to 48 per cent fat, so the calf can grow a thick, warm layer of **blubber** as quickly as possible. The calf begins to eat some solid food at three to four months old, but may be nursed by its mother for one or even two years. Young calves eat herring, young salmon and squid, when available.

The calf swims close to the mother. Keeping close like this makes it more difficult for a large shark to single the young orca out as **prey**. When the calf begins to communicate, it uses sounds similar to the calls of its mother.

Calves of **resident** orcas will spend their entire life with their pod, swimming, hunting and feeding alongside their mother, sisters, brothers, cousins, aunts, uncles, grandmother and sometimes even great-grandmother.

Orca birth rates

Female orcas cannot breed until they are six to ten years old. They continue to produce calves every four to five years for the next twenty years or so. Twins are rare, but have been seen in the wild. Males mature later than females and are able to breed at between twelve and sixteen years of age. This low **birth rate** means that orca **populations** take a long time to recover from a decline in numbers, especially as half of newborn orcas die in their first year.

An orca calf surfaces near its mother. A calf may stay very close to its mother, learning from her constantly, for up to ten years.

Toxic chemicals in the sea

Humans have created around 80,000 new chemicals in the last 50 years. These **synthetic** chemicals have **contaminated** the air, rivers and seas all over the world. Even really remote regions, like the Arctic, are now polluted by dangerous **toxic** chemicals, which have arrived there through the air and by sea.

Long-lived poisons

Chemicals like PCBs and DDT do not disappear quickly once put into the sea, but remain in the environment for a long time, poisoning the water over many years.

The chemicals

PCBs (polychlorinated biphenyls) were invented in 1929 and used to cool and oil electrical equipment. In 1977 PCBs were banned in Canada, the USA, Europe and Australia because they are so poisonous. However by that time PCBs had already been dumped in the seas worldwide. PCBs are dangerous because they can damage the nervous system and the development of young animals, including orcas. Humans are still pouring many other poisonous substances into the world's oceans, such as **pesticides** like DDT and **crude oil**. DDT can cause death to animals by poisoning. It can also cause various cancers and may interfere with **breeding** in orcas.

A ship discharges waste into Pearl Harbor, Hawaii, USA. The illegal dumping of poisonous waste from ships is still a big environmental problem around the world.

Oil spills often mean disaster for wildlife and the environment. Here, people clean up oil that has washed up on to a beach following the Exxon Valdez accident in Alaska in 1989.

Problems in the food chain

Toxic chemicals and substances like lead and mercury cause big problems in the ocean's **food chain**. The animals that live in the sea take in these poisons with their food. Because the poisons are stored in their body fat, they get passed on as one animal eats another. As a **predator** at the top of the food chain, the orca receives very high levels of these **pollutants** through its food. They are also passed on to young whales as they develop inside their mother's body, and later too, through their mother's milk.

Another species of whale called the beluga, has recently been closely studied in Canada. Scientists found that PCBs in their bodies had lowered their **birth rate** and made them more likely to catch diseases. Worryingly, recent tests carried out off Washington state, USA have shown that orcas there have four to five times more of these harmful PCBs in their bodies than the belugas in the Canadian study. This makes them some of the most contaminated animals on Earth.

Disaster at sea

On a clear, sunny day in March 1989, the *Exxon Valdez* oil tanker grounded, spilling crude oil into the waters of Prince William Sound in Alaska. The damage to wildlife was huge and some **species**, such as the harbour seal, still show little or no sign of recovery. In 1989–90 one orca **pod** living in the area suddenly decreased in number from 36 to 22 whales. No young orcas were born in the pod immediately after the oil spill, although since 1995 numbers in the pod have been slowly rising again, reaching 26 orcas in 2001.

Noise pollution and boats

Orcas, like other **cetaceans**, have very sensitive hearing and live in a world full of sound. Even without human activities, the ocean can be a surprisingly noisy place. The moans and hums made by blue whales, for example, are the loudest noises made by any creature on Earth and carry for thousands of kilometres across the oceans. Fish and **marine mammals** make a variety of sounds and even heavy rain adds to the noise levels underwater.

Orcas surface alongside an oil refinery in New Zealand. Oil rigs and oil exploration make a lot of underwater noise.

Humans have added greatly to underwater noise levels in recent years. Large ships, tankers and speedboats are some of the main causes of increased noise in the sea. Drilling for oil, exercises by military boats and seal scarers that fishermen use to keep seals away from their nets also help to create what is called **noise pollution**. Scientists now believe that noise pollution is affecting the **echolocation** signals that cetaceans use to communicate with each other and locate their **prey**.

Noisy waters

Because orcas use sound to find and catch their prey, too much noise underwater forces them to swim harder and longer to find their prey, and so they use up more energy. Eventually they need to make use of the energy stored in the layer of fat, called **blubber**, under their skin. Studies on whales in Puget Sound have found that they are now using nearly 20 per cent more energy than they did before whale-watching became popular there.

Whale-watchers

Whale-watching boats take people out to sea to watch whales for pleasure. However, these boats can also cause noise pollution and other problems for the orcas, interfering with their hunting, resting and family activities for example. Sometimes large numbers of boats go out to watch the same group of whales. For example, in Puget Sound in north-west USA, there are often up to 100 whale-watching boats out at sea at the height of the season. Orcas also face the danger of being hit by boats or their propellers and this can cause serious injury, or even death. A large number of orcas in New Zealand waters have suffered in this way.

Modern hunting

In Greenland people now use motorboats instead of canoes for seal hunting. It is possible that the decline in orcas in this area over recent years has been caused in part by the noise pollution

If whale-watching boats get too close or approach too fast, they can cause orcas unnecessary stress and harm.

Smelly fumes

When there are many boats at sea, exhaust fumes can collect over the surface of the water. When orcas come up to take a breath of fresh air, they take in smelly exhaust fumes instead. The effects of breathing polluted air have not been scientifically studied in orcas, but this must be very unhealthy for them.

Food shortages

Human activities are reducing the types of food that orcas and other **marine** predators like to eat. Chinook salmon are a major part of the **diet** of **resident** orcas off the coast of Washington state, USA. Recently the number of salmon here has declined, partly because people are taking too many fish from the water. This is called **overfishing**.

As in other developed parts of the world, people living in Washington state need more and more energy and water (energy to run street lights and computers; water to wash cars, sprinkle the garden or take a bath). To cope with the demand, large dams have been built across the rivers to generate **hydroelectric power**. In 2001, a drought year, the cities used up so much of the water from the rivers that 1.6 million young salmon were stranded and died and 150,000 fish had to be taken by truck to their final destination.

Changes in the food chain

In the Crozet Archipelago, the orca's main **prey** are southern elephant seals and **baleen** whales. In the past, human hunting of whales here caused baleen whale **populations** to drop and they have not recovered. The population of elephant seals here also declined between 1970 and 1990 and remains at a low level for reasons that scientists do not yet understand. Here again, orcas are facing a shortage of food.

*Dams like this one in the state of Washington, USA, can prevent salmon from swimming upstream to breed. Fewer breeding salmon mean less food for **predators** like orcas.*

Changes in the **food chain** are affecting orcas in Alaska and the Aleutian Islands. Here seals and sea lions are an important part of the orca's diet, but their numbers are falling. In 1977 a sudden rise in water temperatures in the Gulf of Alaska led to a reduction in **plankton** and the animals that feed on them. This had a harmful effect further up the food chain resulting in declines in the numbers of seals and sea lions, and so less food for orcas.

Hungry orcas

When orcas are hungry and short of food they begin to use their **blubber** reserves as food. In doing so, they release any poisons that may be present into their bloodstream. Along with the food shortages themselves, this is another threat to orcas today.

Salmon tumble down on to the deck of a fishing boat in Alaska. Overfishing in parts of North America is causing food shortages for orcas.

Increase in fisheries

Commercial fisheries are now seriously affecting food chains in the sea. Since the 1970s, these fisheries have dramatically increased the number of fish they catch. The number of commercial fishing boats worldwide has doubled since 1970 and fishing techniques have become more destructive. As much as 25 per cent of the fish caught are just thrown away because they too small or of no commercial value. Many fish **species** are greatly reduced in numbers by overfishing, and predators such as orcas are getting short of food.

Whaling and orcas

Humans have used whale meat and oil from whale **blubber** for many centuries. Orcas were once hunted on a small scale by **native** peoples on the west coast of the USA. This is called **subsistence** hunting and still takes place in Greenland and Papua New Guinea in the southwest Pacific Ocean. Because only small numbers of whales are killed in subsistence hunting, it does not have a serious effect on whale **populations**.

Commercial whaling, on the other hand, is whale hunting carried out to make money. Since its boom time around 1900, whaling has led to massive falls in the numbers of whales of different **species** around the world.

A ban on whaling?

In 1946 the International Whaling Commission was set up to control whaling and 40 years later, in 1986, commercial whaling was banned. However, despite this ruling, Norway and Japan still continue to hunt whales commercially, although they do not take as many whales as in the past. Iceland started whaling again in 2003.

A minke whale is hauled aboard a whaling boat in the Barents Sea, Norway. Minke whales are among the most hunted whale species today.

Large quantities of whale meat are still eaten in Japan and Norway. This pile of whale meat chunks is on sale in Japan.

Meat and oil

Whales are hunted commercially for their meat and oil. Because orcas are not as big as other whales, they have not really been hunted commercially for their oil (21 orcas are needed to produce as much oil as one sperm whale, for example). However, orcas have been hunted in several regions around the world for their meat. For instance, Norwegian whalers killed around 56 orcas each year from 1938–81. In the 1979–80 whaling season, the Soviet Union killed over 900 orcas in the Antarctic in just one year. Orcas are still killed today by whalers when they are hunting other species.

Conflict with fishermen

Fishermen have often killed or ill-treated orcas because they thought that whales competed for the fish they were trying to catch. This led to many orca deaths in the Icelandic and Norwegian herring fisheries. The killing of orcas by fishermen is still a serious problem, particularly where orcas take fish straight from fishing nets, such as in Alaska. Fishermen in the Crozet Archipelago in the Indian Ocean use illegal explosives to frighten away orcas from their fishing nets and lines.

Whale products

For centuries whales have been hunted for their oil and meat. Some of the uses for whale products have included margarine and cooking oil (from whale oil), corsets and umbrellas (from whalebone or **baleen**), fertilizer (from ground-up whale bones), and string for tennis racquets (from whale tendons). The sperm whale was hunted for a special kind of oil found in its head. This was used in lamp oil, as well as in candles, soaps, cosmetics and perfume.

Orca strandings

Every year thousands of whales, dolphins and porpoises are found stranded on beaches around the world. Some **cetaceans** die at sea and are washed up on to the shore, others are alive when stranded and become trapped in shallow waters. Cetaceans may be washed ashore alone or in groups, known as mass strandings. Cetaceans beached on the shore usually die within a few hours or days if not given help.

Orca strandings are not as common as those of some other **species**, such as sperm whales, which frequently strand and often in groups. Usually it is male orcas that are stranded, although the reason for this is unknown. New Zealand has one of the highest rates of orca stranding in the world. Over 70 have been stranded there since 1860, and in recent years there has been a stranding every two years on average. The high rate of live orca strandings in New Zealand may be a result of the whales' liking for rays that live in the shallow waters there.

Orcas are also frequently stranded on the Argentine coast when chasing **prey**, such as sea lions, on to the shore.

A group of long-finned pilot whales have stranded on a beach. Rescuers keep them wet by hosing them with water and covering their skin to prevent sunburn.

Helping a stranded cetacean

If you find a stranded whale or dolphin it is important to telephone an expert for help as soon as possible. Many countries have 'stranding networks' of people who are specially trained in dealing with stranded **marine mammals**. Always keep other people and dogs away from a stranded cetacean to reduce stress to the animal.

An orca has been left high and dry by the retreating tide on a New Zealand beach. A team of whale rescue volunteers in this country has saved the lives of thousands of cetaceans stranded around the coastline.

Live animals that have stranded alone are often old, injured, sick or have lost their sense of direction. Mass strandings may occur because either the animal that is leading the rest of the group has made a mistake in **navigation** or has become sick or wounded and led the rest of its **pod** on to the shore. However in many cases scientists do not know the reasons for cetaceans beaching on the shore and many animals appear to be healthy. It is also not understood why stranded whales that have been rescued and pulled back into deeper water will often immediately return to strand themselves again on the same stretch of beach.

Research and protection

Because wild orcas spend almost their entire lives underwater, they are difficult to study. The dead bodies of whales do provide valuable information for scientists, but while some dead orcas are washed ashore, most sink to the seabed and are never seen again.

Learning everything we can about orcas so that we can understand them better is one of the best ways to protect them and plan their **conservation**. Scientists are now studying them closely to try and find out, for example, why half of all newborn orcas die in their first year, whether increased boat traffic is seriously affecting whale behaviour and exactly how **toxic** chemicals are affecting their health.

This leaping orca has a coloured radio tag attached to its back behind its dorsal fin. These tags are important in whale research and can record information, such as swimming speed and diving depths.

Tagging orcas

One of the methods used to research and record orca behaviour is the time-depth recording tag. Scientists attach these tags to stranded orcas before they are returned to the sea and they can provide valuable information. The tags are made to drop off after a while and float to the water's surface. A tag found on a beach in Washington state, USA, had been fixed to a male orca stranded nearby two weeks earlier. The tag had recorded the orca's swimming speed, the depth to which it had been diving and how often it surfaced, all of which indicated that it was doing well.

Well-studied orcas

Having been studied for 30 years, the northern and southern **resident** orcas off the west coast of the USA are amongst the best-researched whales in the world. Research programmes have also been carried out on orcas in the Crozet Archipelago in the Indian Ocean, as well as in New Zealand and Argentina.

A pod of orcas swims near a whale research boat off the Lofoten Islands in Norway. Research into orca populations and behaviour is very important for their future.

Orca protection

Killer whales are listed as conservation dependent by the World Conservation Union. This is the international conservation group that is responsible for listing all plant and animal **species** that are thought to be at risk. Conservation dependent means that the orcas are the focus of a special conservation programme. If this programme is stopped, the species would be listed as threatened within five years and the future survival of the species would actually be at risk.

Radio Orca!

Researchers have discovered a great deal of information about orca communication by listening to the sounds they make. Underwater sounds can be heard and recorded using a special underwater microphone, called a hydrophone. In Johnstone Strait, British Columbia, on the Canadian coast, the world's first whale radio station, ORCA-FM, was launched in July 1998. The whistles, whines and squeals made by the orcas moving through the Strait can be heard live 24 hours a day within several kilometres of this radio station.

How sightings can help orcas

Sightings schemes

There are now several whale sightings schemes in which the public can take part, organized by groups like the Whale and Dolphin Conservation Society and the Orca Research Trust (New Zealand).

These researchers are carrying out whale survey work. Although cetaceans may often be found in the same waters all year round, they are usually easiest to find on calm days in clear, sunny weather.

Observing whales from the shore or from boats and gathering scientific information about them is an important part of whale research. Information such as which whale species was seen, how many whales, what they were doing and where the sighting had taken place is all noted down. Whale sighting is different from whale-watching: while sightings gather important information, whale-watching is usually organized for groups of tourists.

Value to research?

Sightings of **cetaceans**, including orcas, off the coasts of the USA, Canada, Europe, Australia and New Zealand are increasing as more people are becoming aware of whales and dolphins and are looking out for them.

Every reported sighting, whether it is from on land or from a boat, can be valuable to whale scientists. The information from sightings is gathered together and put on to computers. Building an accurate picture of orca movements helps scientists to find out how many whales there are in an area, and where they are in the world's oceans.

Orca dorsal fins

male   female

Male or female?

You can tell whether an orca is a male or female quite easily by the shape and size of its dorsal fin. The male's dorsal fin can be as tall as a human (almost 2 metres high) and is the tallest dorsal fin in the animal kingdom! It is more upright and triangular than the female's dorsal fin, which is usually up to 1.2 metres high, and curved backwards.

Identifying killer whales

With their distinctive black and white patterning, huge rounded head and tall **dorsal fin**, orcas are easy to spot when they emerge from the water. Even if they only partly surface, you can usually see the dorsal fin and shape of the head. Another helpful feature for recognizing orcas is the shape of the blow, or spout — the cloud of moist air that whales breathe out from their blowhole.

Scientists can easily identify individual orcas by using photographs. Each orca has a light grey patch behind the dorsal fin, known as a saddle patch. It is different in shape and size in every animal. Orcas usually also have scars or nicks on the dorsal fins or distinctive white eye patches. These features are photographed and catalogued and can be used by scientists to follow individual orcas throughout their lives.

An orca's blow is a fine spray about 3 metres in height, wide and rounded in shape, rather like a bush. It often makes an explosive sound and is a useful way of recognizing orcas at sea.

Reducing toxic chemicals

In our daily lives we depend on the use of hundreds of different **synthetic** chemicals — for example in plastics, cosmetics, cleaning fluids, food preservatives, **pesticides** and even computers.

There are very good reasons why we need to reduce the amounts of chemicals we produce and use, because some of them are very poisonous to wildlife and also to ourselves. For instance, PCBs were once thought to be harmless, but they are still having harmful effects on animals, including orcas, around the world.

Even beaches on remote islands are often littered with rubbish, sometimes brought long distances by ocean currents.

Don't be a litter bug!

The litter we drop on beaches, particularly plastics and drinks cans, can harm **marine** wildlife if they try to eat it or get tangled up in it. When having a party outside, keep all balloons carefully tied down. They look very pretty floating off up into the sky, but they will eventually burst and end up as plastic litter on land or in the sea, where they may be mistakenly swallowed by animals.

Action needed!

Conservation groups believe the risks to the environment — our land, rivers, oceans and the air we breathe — are so high that we should all take action now to reduce our use of **toxic** chemicals. Conservation groups like WWF (Worldwide Fund for Nature) are campaigning for new laws that will stop the use of long-lasting chemicals. To reduce the threat from toxic chemicals, governments and the public all over the world will need to play a part. The good news is that it is possible to reverse the damaging effects of these chemicals over time.

Making a difference

We can all do something to help. We can avoid the use of pesticides in the home and garden for example, and use cleaning products that do not harm the environment. We can buy soap, shampoos and cosmetics that do not contain synthetic perfumes, and use paints, varnishes and glues that are based on water

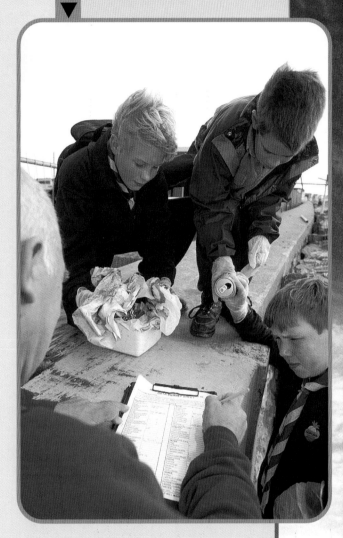

and not synthetic chemicals. Organic farming avoids the use of harmful chemicals such as pesticides, and is gentle on the environment. You can find out more about this from groups like the Soil Association.

It is a good idea to find out where your water comes from and where it goes once you have used it, and never pour any paints or synthetic chemicals down the drain. **Pollutants** can travel down to the sea through our rivers and streams and have harmful effects on marine life. If you are unsure about what to do with any dangerous or poisonous waste, like used car oil for example, contact your local environment agency.

Protecting food supplies

As we have seen, our own huge demands for water and energy along with the practice of **overfishing**, are all affecting the orca's food supply. Off the coast of Washington state in the USA, for example, chinook salmon have been decreasing in numbers, leaving orcas short of their main source of food.

Water and energy

Conservation groups in the area are now encouraging people to cut their use of water and energy in order to restore the river levels and the salmon. Over a quarter of all water used in a typical house here, is used merely to flush the lavatory! There are now water-saving devices that can help lessen the amount of water used in lavatories, washing machines and showers.

Of course, it is important to preserve water and cut down on the energy we use wherever we live: it all adds up to helping the environment. Advice on how to make homes more energy efficient and how to insulate them better is often free from energy supply companies. Putting weather strips around doors and windows, for example, helps plug leaks and prevents the escape of heat energy. Replacing standard light bulbs with compact fluorescent bulbs also saves large amounts of energy. Water heaters that use **solar power** to provide hot water can cut the use of **hydroelectric power**. (Bathing accounts for the third largest use of indoor water and the second highest use of energy in parts of Washington state.)

*These steps were built for fish! This is a fish ladder in Oregon, USA, built next to a big dam. The ladder enables salmon in the river to bypass the dam and continue their journey upstream to **breed**.*

A salmon leaps out of the sea to try to escape a hunting orca. Here, off the Canadian coast, the salmon are plentiful and there is a healthy orca population.

Helping the salmon

People are now working hard to restore salmon **habitat** along the rivers in Washington state by planting trees and shrubs along the riverbanks. This will provide better shade, reduce water temperature, and prevent banks from collapsing, making the rivers more suitable for salmon to breed. It all helps orca conservation too. Fishermen are being encouraged to give up fishing for salmon altogether, or at least avoid fishing in **Marine** Protected Areas, where fish **populations** are being helped to recover.

Salmon and orcas

Salmon are remarkable fish that are born in freshwater streams inland. They swim down to the sea to mature and eventually return to the same stream where they were born, to breed. They may travel as far as 1600 kilometres (nearly 1000 miles) from sea to river to lay their eggs, after which they usually die. During the years that they spend maturing in the sea, salmon travel thousands of kilometres all around the northern Pacific Ocean from Washington to Alaska, Japan and Russia. Orcas catch salmon in coastal waters either soon after they have left their freshwater streams when young or as they return to breed.

Whale-watching and orcas

Commercial whale-watching for pleasure began in the 1950s. Nowadays, there are many companies that offer tourists the chance to watch whales and dolphins in the wild all over the world. Trips on whale-watching boats can last just one hour or up to two weeks.

Harm or help?

Whale-watching can cause harm to whales if there are too many boats or if it is done carelessly, since **cetaceans** can then suffer from **noise pollution** or may even collide with boats. This is happening on some trips around San Juan Island in Puget Sound, USA.

On the other hand, if carried out responsibly, whale-watching can help orca **conservation** through the interest it creates in people. Whale-watching provides fantastic opportunities to see these animals in the wild. As the orca is a particularly spectacular, active and acrobatic **species**, it is very popular with whale watchers.

Spot the orca! Children watch orcas from the deck of a whale-watching boat off the coast of Washington state, USA. Their boat is keeping well back from the orcas in order not to upset them.

A whale-watching trip is an unforgettable experience! Educational talks and commentaries during the trips help to raise people's awareness and inspire them to help care for the **marine** environment and the wildlife, such as orcas, that live there. Whale-watch operators in many parts of the world are also in a good position to carry out valuable research and that is benefiting the whales too.

Big business

Whale-watching is booming business: Iceland earned over £3.5 million from whale-watching in 1997. Income from whale-watching has become important to coastal communities such as Provincetown in Massachusetts, USA, Tofino in British Columbia, Canada and Monkey Mia in Australia. The benefit to whales is that responsible whale-watching makes money from these animals without harming them. This means that if whales are properly protected, whale-watching can provide coastal communities of people with a good, long-term income.

*Whale researchers use whale-watching boat trips to carry out their orca studies. The shape of the **dorsal fins** is often used to help identify individual orcas.*

Whale-watching Code of Conduct

This is the whale- and dolphin-watching Code of Conduct and should be followed by all whale-watching boat operators:

· keep your distance. Never go closer than 100 metres (200 metres if another boat is present)
· never drive head on to, or move between, scatter or separate cetaceans. If unsure of their movements, simply stop and put the engine into neutral
· spend no longer than 15 minutes near the animals
· take special care with mothers and young
· maintain a steady direction and keep speeds low
· never try to swim with wild cetaceans, for your safety and theirs
· don't dispose of any rubbish or litter at sea.

Orcas in marine parks

Whales and dolphins, including orcas, are kept in **marine** parks and aquariums around the world. Most sea-living **mammals** in captivity, including orcas, have been taken from the wild. Over 130 orcas have been captured for aquariums and marine parks since 1961. Waters off the north-west coast of the USA and Iceland once provided many orcas for this purpose, before the capture of live orcas was banned there. Some orcas have been caught recently in Japanese waters for marine parks in Japan, and the Russian government gave permission to catch ten live orcas off their east coast in 2003.

Problems of live capture

Scientists do not yet fully understand the effects of capture upon wild **populations** of orcas or upon individual animals. Capturing a mother orca will affect young that still depend on her. Removing a young orca means the **pod** has lost an animal that can **breed** in future, and this may harm the pod since orcas have such low **birth rates**.

Scientists believe that whales can become stressed during capture and when transported. In nature the orca is a wild animal that lives in groups and swims in open seas. In captivity an orca's surroundings are very different: it is confined in a small space near noisy humans, and since hunting real **prey** is no longer possible, it is given dead fish to eat.

After capture orcas become tame and can easily be taught to perform tricks and spectacular acrobatics for the crowds.

Keiko's story

Keiko was captured by fishermen in Icelandic waters in 1979 when he was two years old. In captivity he became a performing animal and in 1992 starred in the popular movie *Free Willy*. When people found out about his poor health and living conditions, Keiko was moved to an aquarium in the USA for two years. Here he was brought back to good health. Once fit again, Keiko went to an enclosure on the Icelandic coast where his keepers began to prepare him for release back into the wild. When released in 2002, he swam from Iceland to Norway, where he became so popular that he had to be moved to a more remote bay. Keepers fed him there, but he was free to roam. Sadly, in December 2003, Keiko suddenly became ill and died.

Benefits to orcas?

Until around 25 years ago orcas were widely feared and misunderstood. Watching these whales in captivity has improved the orca's image among the public and they are now widely appreciated as intelligent animals rather than cruel **predators**. Seeing orcas at close quarters is also hugely popular and is an experience that most people would never be able to enjoy otherwise. Many people also think that parks can have a valuable educational role.

Keiko's capture and release into the wild were very controversial and many people have mixed feelings about it.

How can you help?

Orcas are facing many serious threats today all over the world, and the task of helping them may seem very difficult. In fact there is a lot you can do to help.

Adopt an orca

Try taking part in an 'Adopt a whale' programme. By adopting an orca you will be helping to support research of orcas in the wild which is vital for their **conservation**. There are several schemes: the Adopt a Whale Programme run by WDCS, the Whale and Dolphin Conservation Society, the Orca Adoption Programme in the USA, the BC Wild Killer Whale Adoption Programme in Canada, or the Adopt an Orca projects in the USA and New Zealand. You can often choose which orca you would like to adopt from photographs that are available online. In return you will receive a photograph of 'your' whale and be kept up-to-date with all the latest news on orca research.

Take part!

You can also get involved by joining a whale conservation organization and actively taking part in their campaigns. You will receive regular newsletters or magazines letting you know about the charity's work and updates on whale conservation. You may be able to join in interesting events organized by the charity. Try emailing or writing a letter to your elected government representative about the threats to orcas. Your MP has a duty to listen and has the power to inform government about important conservation issues.

Adopting a whale is a great way to help conserve orcas and other whales. You can find out more about adopting whales by contacting groups like the WDCS, The Whale and Dolphin Conservation Society.

High numbers of orcas are a sign that our seas are healthy, so helping to conserve whales is not only good for them, it benefits our environment and local communities too.

Whale sightings

Taking part in whale sighting schemes is also of great value to orca research. Schemes are organized by WDCS, the Whale and Dolphin Conservation Society, Adopt an Orca and the Whale Museum (USA). Whale-watching tours are among the most exciting wildlife experiences on Earth! There are opportunities to take part in the UK, US, Australia, New Zealand and in many other countries around the world. Just make sure your boat operator follows the whale-watching code first. Then you can really enjoy watching orcas and other **cetaceans** too and learn more about these wonderful animals.

Raising funds

You can raise money for charities working for orca or whale conservation by holding an orca raffle, or organizing a boot sale or school jumble sale, for instance.

Read on

Finally, you can find out much more about the fascinating world of orcas and other cetaceans and the threats to their survival by looking up information on the internet and reading books.

Glossary

baleen comb-like structure made of keratin in a whale's mouth that filters food from the water

birth rate number of young produced by an animal over a fixed time period

blubber layer of fat under the skin of marine mammals

breed produce young

cetacean mammal that spends its entire life in water. Cetaceans need to come to the surface regularly to breathe air and have one or two nostrils, or blowholes.

commercial done to make money

conservation work done to protect wild plants and animals and their habitats

contaminate pollute

crude oil oil that has not yet been purified for use

diet food an animal eats

dorsal fin fin located on the back of a fish or whale

echolocation detection of objects using high-frequency sound waves, used by some animals, including orcas, to locate prey or find their way about

ecosystem all the plants and animals in an area together with their non-living environment

endothermic warm-blooded; maintaining a more or less constant body temperature that is largely independent of the temperature of the environment

estuary river mouth, where fresh water and sea water meet

fluke broad flat tail fins of cetaceans

food chain series of living things each forming food (and so providing energy) for the next living thing in the chain

habitat place where a plant or animal naturally lives

hydroelectric power energy generated from the power of falling water in rivers or streams

mammal warm-blooded animal that feeds its young with milk from its body

marine living in the sea. Marine parks are wildlife parks where marine animals are kept.

mucus slimy, slippery substance produced by some living organisms

native   belonging to a particular country or place

navigation   method of finding out where you are on land or sea

noise pollution   sound that is harmful to humans or wildlife

nutrient   substance that provides nourishment

overfishing   taking too many fish from the sea

parasite   animal that lives on or inside another animal's body. Large numbers can cause illness.

pectoral fin   side fin

pesticide   substance that kills pests, such as wasps and flies and is usually synthetic

plankton   tiny forms of life that live in the seas, lakes and rivers

pod   social group of whales

polar   area within the Arctic or Antarctic Circles

pollutant   substance that causes pollution

pollution   presence of high levels of harmful substances in the environment, often put there by human activity

population   group of living things of the same species within a particular area

predator   animal that hunts or kills another animal for food

prey   animal hunted or killed by another animal for food

resident   living in one place. Resident orcas stay in one area in close family groups.

solar power   energy from the Sun

species   particular type of animal or other living thing. Orcas are a species of whale.

subsistence   what is needed to support life

synthetic   not naturally occurring, but made by humans

toxic   poisonous

transient   not living in one place all the time

tropical   area lying close to the equator where the climate is moist and very warm

Conservation groups and websites

All the organizations below are working to help protect orcas and other cetaceans through campaigns and education. You can find out much more about them by visiting their websites.

WWF

www.panda.org

Formerly known as the World Wildlife Fund, the WWF is an international charity that takes action to protect threatened species and tackle global threats to the environment for the benefit of people and nature. The WWF has branches in many countries around the world. Their website has lots of information and some fun games to play too.

Whale and Dolphin Conservation Society

www.wdcs.org

International charity that works in over 20 countries for the conservation of whales, dolphins and their environment. The WDCS also runs an Adopt a Whale scheme.

American Cetacean Society

www.acsonline.org

Charity in the USA that works to protect whales, dolphins and porpoises and their habitats through education, conservation and research.

Soil Association

www.soilassociation.org

Organization campaigning for organic food and farming.

Other useful websites:

Whale Times

www.whaletimes.org

Website all about whales aimed at children. Includes a very useful dictionary of whale words and invites questions about whales via email.

Orca adoption schemes are run by the following organizations:

The Whale Museum
www.whalemuseum.org

Orca Research Trust
in New Zealand *www.orca.org.nz*
and in USA *www.orca.nz/usa.htm*

British Columbia Wild Killer Whale Adoption Program
www.killerwhale.org

Books

Animal Groups: Life in a Pod – Whales, Richard and Louise Spilsbury
(Heinemann Library, 2003)

Green Alert: Polluted Waters, Jennifer Stefanow (Raintree, 2004)

Killer Whales, Mark Cawardine (BBC Books, 2001)

Orca. The Whale Called Killer, Erich Hoyt (Camden House, 1995)

Orca. Visions of the Killer Whale, Peter Knudtson
(Douglas and McIntyre, 1996)

Whales, Peter Evans, (Whittet Books, 1990)

Videos

The Blue Planet: A Natural History of the Oceans, narrated by David
Attenborough (BBC, 2001)

Killer Whales: Wolves of the Sea, narrated by David Attenborough
(National Geographic, 1993)

Index

Titles in the *Animals under Threat* series include:

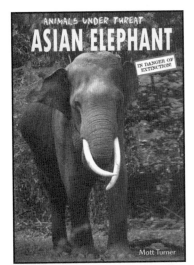

Hardback   0 431 18902 1

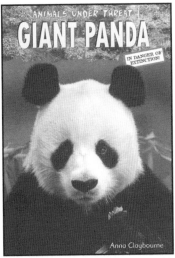

Hardback   0 431 18903 X

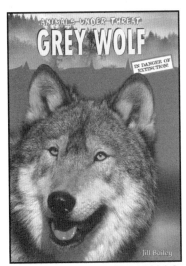

Hardback   0 431 18904 8

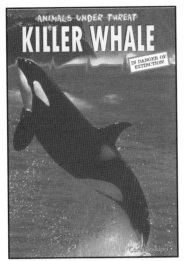

Hardback   0 431 18905 6

Hardback   0 431 18906 4

Hardback   0 431 18907 2

Find out about the other titles in this series on our website www.heinemann.co.uk/library